DMV

Practice Test made Easy

Over 150 Questions on practice test, written exams, license permit, study and guide book

By Wince .N. George

Copyright

TABLE OF CONTENT

Chapter One

Permit Practice Test 1

1. One of the following is an excellent example of defensive driving

   a) Keep an eye on the cars brake lights in front of you while driving

   b) Keep your eyes moving in search of potential risks

   c) Keep an eye on a car behind you and the car in front of you.

   d) None of the above

Answer B

2 What do you do as soon as you get to the railroad crossing with no signals?

   a) Stop completely

   b) Slow down and be ready to stop.

   c) Speed to get through the tracks quickly.

   d) None of the above.

Answer B

3. When driving on roads that are wet you should

   a) Increase your speed

b) Reduce your speed

c) Pump your breaks occasionally

d) Switch to low beam headlights

Answer B

4. Keep your eyes steady on the road, quickly change to neutral, pull off the road when clear to do so and turn off the engine are things you do for?

a) A tire blowout.

b) Power failure.

c) Headlight failure.

d) A stuck gas pedal.

Answer D

5. **What is the major cause of most rear-end collisions?**

a) Failing to inspect the vehicle.

b) Not looking at your mirrors.

c) Discussing with passengers

d) Following too close

Answer D

6. The **highest speed you can apply in a residential or business area when there is no speed limit displayed is**

    a)   30 mph

    b)   25 mph

    c)   35 mph

    d)   40 mph

Answer B

7. Except if a sign stops you, when may you turn left at a red light?

    a)   In the case of an emergency.

    b)   Coming from a two- way road to a one -way road.

    c)   Moving from a one- way road to a one- way road.

    d)   Not at all

Answer C

8. The most effective way to avoid collision is

    a)   Your lights should be on at all times.

    b)   Wearing a seat belt.

    c)   Keeping a moderate space between vehicles at all times.

d) Driving slowly at all times.

Answer C

9. It is prohibited to follow fire vehicles going in response to an alarm, within

a) 500 feet distance

b) 200 feet distance

c) 300 feet distance

d) 400 feet distance

Answer A

10. If you are driving on a highway posted for 65 mph and the traffic is traveling at 70 mph, what maximum speed will you drive legally?

a) Follow the speed of traffic.

b) Drive between 65 mph and 70 mph.

c) Increase your speed to pass other traffic.

d) Don't go faster than 65 mph.

Answer D

11. When is the road most slippery when it is raining?

a) When it started to rain first

b) After it has been raining for some time.

c) When the rain has stopped, but the road is still very wet.

d) None of the above.

12. Seeing and scanning an event well in advance will help to prevent

a) Fatigue

b) Distractions

c) Panic stops

d) Lane changes

13. When should you obey a construction flagger's directives?

a) Only when you see it is required to do so.

b) If they do not go against existing signs or signals.

c) If they are wearing a state or federal badge.

d) All the time in construction zones.

Answer D

14. What type of drugs can affect your capability to drive safely?

a) All drugs, prescription or over the counter drugs, can affect your ability to drive.

b) Alcohol, marijuana, and Cocaine

c) Illegal drugs only

d) None of the above

Answer A

15. Anytime you hear or see an emergency vehicle approaching, what should you do?

a) Move your car immediately to the right side of the road and come to a stop

b) Slow down and allow the emergency vehicle to pass

c) Remain watchful and stay to the right

d) Ignore and speed off.

Answer A

16. Before you enter a road from an alley, lane or driveway, you must

    a) Flash your car high beam headlights

    b) Sound or honk your horn

    c) Stop before getting to the sidewalk

    d) Enter without doing anything

Answer C

17. What is the meaning of a white painted curb?

    a) Passengers or freight. Loading zone

    b) No loading zone.

    c) Passengers or Mail loading zone

    d) No loitering.

Answer C

18. What does an orange sign?

    a) State highway ahead.

    b) Merging lanes ahead.

    c) Construction work ahead.

    d) There is divided highway ahead.

19 The car that made an accurate turn was

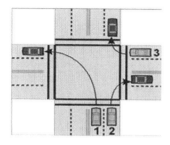

a) Car 2

b) Car 1

c) Car 3

d) Car 2 and 3

20. When you want to make a turn, use your turn signs

a) For a minimum of 500 feet

b) For a minimum of 4 seconds

c) Only when you can see other vehicles on the road

d) For almost 2 seconds

21. In which condition is it ok to back up on the highway?

a) If you pass your exit because of oversight.

b) To go back to see an accident.

c) When picking up someone on the side of the highway.

d) It is not ok to back up on the highway.

Answer D

22 The wheelchair sign in a parking space means that it is set aside for incapacitated individuals

a) Any driver can use it, if there is no available space

b) For loading and offloading

c) With no exceptions

d) For waiting

Answer C

23. **When you come close to a school bus that is dropping off or picking up children, you must**

    a)   Stop and then gently drive with caution

    b)   Stop until the bus start moving or the stop signal arm is no longer stretched

    c)   Slow down and yield the right of way to all pedestrians

    d)   Ignore the sign and continue moving.

Answer B

24. **Which lane will you use on a freeway if you are driving faster than other traffic?**

    a)   Lane on the right.

    b)   The shoulder.

    c)   Lane on the left.

    d)   The carpool lane.

Answer C

25. How distant ahead should you look when driving on the highway?

  a) 1 city block.

  b) 1 quarter mile.

  c) 1 half mile.

  d) 1 mile.

Answer B

26. Traffic lanes going in opposite directions are separated by what color lines.

  a) White

  b) Red

  c) Orange.

  d) Yellow

Answer D

27. When driving and you are stopped by law enforcement, you should

  a) Park the car and remain in the vehicle

  b) Keep your seat belt fastened and put your hand on a steering wheel in a visible location

c) Ignore and zoom off.

d) A and B above.

Answer D

28. As you approach an intersection and you noticed that the traffic light has changed from green to yellow. What will be your reaction?

a) Ignore and stop in the intersection.

b) Hurry up to beat the light before it turns red.

c) Keep moving at your current speed.

d) Stop before the intersection.

Answer D

29. When you want to merge with traffic, at what speed will you enter the traffic

a) A slower speed compared to the traffic.

b) The same speed as traffic.

c) A faster speed compares to the traffic.

d) As fast as you can go.

Answer B

30. Accepting or signing for a citation from a law enforcement officer:

a) Is not an admittance of guilt or obligation?

b) Is an assurance to appear in the case of a criminal violation?

c) All of the above.

d) None of the above.

Answer C

31. How close should you park next to a curb.

a) Not closer than 6 inches coming from the curb.

b) Not further than 6 inches coming from the curb.

c) Not closer than 12 inches coming from the curb.

d) Not further than 18 inches coming from the curb.

Answer D

32. What do you understand by the word 'blind spot'?

a) Blind spots are spaces for blind people to pass at an intersection.

b) Blind spots are marks frequently seen by drivers who have been drinking.

c)   Blind spots are zones near the left and right rear
     corners of your car that is difficult to see with your
     rearview mirrors.

d)   Blind spots are marks seen after gazing into
     oncoming headlights at night.

Answer C

33. When you keep a steady speed and signal in advance when you are about to slow down will help keep what

a)   Your vehicle a safe distance ahead.

b)   A safe distance behind your vehicle.

c)   A safe distance next to your vehicle.

d)   All of the above.

Answer B

34. A lot of lanes of travel in the same direction are demarcated by lane markings of what color?

a)   Red

b)   Yellow

c)   White

d)   Orange

35. If you park a car on an uphill grade, which way would you turn your wheels

    a)   Left

    b)   Right

    c)   Straight

    d)   None

Answer A

36. Dim your high beams each time you come within _____ feet of any approaching vehicle?

    a)   200

    b)   300

    c)   400

    d)   500

Answer D

37. Driving at night is more hazardous than day driving because?

a) The traffic signs are less noticeable at night than day

b) The total distance we can see ahead is reduced.

c) Most People are sleepy at night.

d) Villains come out at nighttime.

Answer B

38. If a tire blows out while on speed, you should

a) Hold the steering wheel steadfastly while you ease up on the gas pedal.

b) Apply the brakes steadily.

c) Shift to neutral and apply the brakes.

d) Ignore, speed up to gain stability, and then pull over.

Answer C

39. A pedestrian using a red or white tipped stick is usually what?

a) A policeman.

b) A construction worker.

c) A blind person.

d) A crossing guard.

40. Anytime you are driving in the rain or snow during the day you should?

a) Use high beams.

b) Use fog lights.

c) Use low beams.

d) Use no headlights.

41. What is the number of alcoholic drink it take to disturb your driving?

a) 1

b) 2

c) 3

d) 4

42. What do a red lighted arrow on a traffic light symbolizes

a) Turning prohibited

b) Stop then wait for the arrow to change to green before turning

c) Stop, observe the traffic light and turn with caution

d) Ignore the traffic light and move ahead

Answer B

43. To dodge the glare from approaching headlights

a) You should focus your eyes on the middle of highway

b) Glance back and forth amid the side of the road and straight.

c) Your eye should be focused on the side of the road

d) Turn your eyes towards the rear

Answer B

44. When do you think you can make a left turn at a traffic green light?

a) If there is a green arrow.

b) On the city streets.

c) After yielding to approaching traffic.

d) On one way streets.

Answer C

45. Which vehicle has the right of way when more than one vehicle stopped at intersection?

a) The main vehicle.

b) The first vehicle that tries to go.

c) The first vehicle to arrive.

d) The vehicle on the right.

Answer C

46. If you are on an intersection when the light changes, you should?

a) Stop in the intersection.

b) Proceed and clear the intersection.

c) Flash your lights through the intersection.

d) Sound your horn through the intersection.

Answer B

47. How to see if there is a car in your blind spot?

a) Lean and look in your mirror back and forth.

b) Look over your shoulder.

c)   Adjust your power mirrors if you possess them.

d)   There is nothing you can do because it is called a blind spot.

Answer B

48. If there is a green light, but traffic is backed up into the intersection, what do you do?

a)   Proceed to the intersection and hope traffic disperses before the light changes.

b)   Hold on until traffic clears before you enter the intersection.

c)   Try to go round the traffic.

d)   Sound your horn to clear the intersection

Answer B

49. At the intersection, a flashing red light means what?

a)   The same as stop sign

b)   Light is about to turn green

c)   None of the above

Answer A

50. A broken white line seen in the center of the road means

a) Traffic on the two sides is moving in the same direction

b) Passing in either direction is prohibited

c) Traffic is flowing in opposite directions

d) There is no traffic in the opposite direction

Answer A

51. If you observe that another driver follows you too closely you should?

a) Slowly speed up.

b) Jam the brakes.

c) Flash your brake lights 3 times.

d) Check if there is room in another lane and move.

Answer D

52. Some of the places you are likely to find slippery spots on the road are

a) In corners and at stop signs.

b)   In overpasses, bridges and shady spots.

c)   On hills and in tunnels.

d)   Near large bodies of water.

Answer B

53. When it begins to get dark and you are driving away from a rising or setting sun on rainy, snowy, or foggy days, it is a good time to?

a)   Look at the tires.
b)   Wear your seatbelt.
c)   Turn on your headlights.
d)   Roll up the windows.

Answer C

54. Before beginning a driving test the state examiner will first check the person's vehicle to:

a)   Make sure that the vehicle has the necessary tools
b)   Make sure that the vehicle is in safe operating situation
c)   Check for Cleanliness
d)   A and B.

Answer D

55. The illustration below shows that the most difficult car for you to see if you are driving in a black car is:

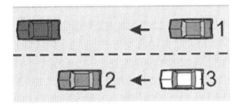

a) Car 3

b) Car 2

c) Car 1

d) Car 1 and2

Answer B

56. When you are about to change lanes, observe your car mirrors for other traffic and

a) Slow down driving by at least one- third

b) Look inside rearview mirror

c) Turn your head rapidly and look over your shoulder

d) Look through your side mirror

Answer C

57. If you are on a freeway and driving faster than other traffic, which lane should you use?

a) The right lane.

b) The shoulder.

c) The left lane.

d) The carpool lane

Answer C

58. Which of the following stimulus the effects of alcohol on the body?

a) Time intervals between each drink.

b) The body weight of a person.

c) The amount of food in the stomach.

d) All of the above.

Answer D

59. Anytime you change an address you are required by law to notify the motor vehicle division within

a) 30 days

b) 10 days

c) 6 months

d) I year

Answer A

60. Keeping a stable speed and signaling in advance when reducing speed or turning will help maintain what

a) A safe distance ahead of your vehicle.

b) A safe distance behind your vehicle.

c) A safe distance next to your vehicle.

d) All of the above.

Answer B

61. What do white painted curbs on the road mean?

a) Loading zone for freight or passengers.

b) No loading zone.

c) Loading zone for passengers or mail.

d) No loitering.

Answer B

62. What should you do when you get at the intersection with a flashing red light?

a) Halt, and then go when safe to do so.

b) Halt and then go when it flashes green.

c) Slow down and give way to any vehicles already in the intersection.

d) Halt and then go when it turns solid green.

Answer A

63. When is the best time to obey instructions from school crossing guards?

a) Only during school hours.

b) Only if you see children present.

c) Only if they are licensed crossing guards.

d) At all times.

Answer D

64. If there is a tire blows out accident you should?

a) Hold firmly the steering wheel while easing up on the gas pedal.

b) Apply the brakes firmly.

c) Shift to neutral and apply the brakes.

d) Speed up for some time to gain stability, and then pull over.

Answer A

65. Seat belts are a must wear for who?

a) The drivers together with all the passengers under the age of 21.

b) The driver, children 8 years of age or older and who are 4 feet 9 inches tall or taller.

c) The driver and the front seat passengers

d) Driver only.

Answer B

66. If more than one vehicle reaches a four-way stop at the same time, which of them will go first?

a) The first one that attempts to go.

b) The one on the left.

c) The one on the right.

d) None of the above.

Answer C

67. When you observe that the traffic light is green and you want to go straight through an intersection. You saw another car is already in the intersection making a turn. You must:

a) Proceed to the intersection and then stop.

b) You have the right of way to drive through the intersection.

c) Allow the car to complete its turn before entering the intersection.

d) None of the above

Answer B

68. If you observe that a traffic light changes from green to yellow as you approach an intersection. What should you do?

a) Keep going at your current speed.

b) Stop before the intersection.

c) Stop, even if in the intersection.

d) Accelerate fast to beat the light before it turns red.

69. What is the correct left-turn hand signal?

a) Hand and arm extended downward.

b) Hand and arm extended out.

c) Hand and arm extended upward.

d) Hand and arm extended up with middle finger

extended upward

Answer B

Chapter Two

DEFENSIVE DRIVING TEST

1. Is it okay to slow down for construction zones and watch out for workers?

    a)   Yes

    b)   No

Answer: A

2. Will you dodge driving in the blind spots of other cars and trucks?

    a)   Yes
    b)   No

Answer: A

3. Are you going to pass other vehicles using the left lanes only?

    a)   Yes

    b)   No

Answer: A

4 Is it okay to drive below the speed limit in poor driving conditions?

    a)   Yes

    b)   No

Answer: A

5. Will you provide a safe cushion of space when coming back over after a lane change?

    a)   Yes

    b)   No

Answer: A

6. Will you use your horn only when necessary?

    a)   Yes

    b)   No

Answer: A

7. Will you avoid using your headlights in an unruly manner?

    a)   Yes

    b)   No

Answer: A

8. Will you pull over to deal with all distractions like phone calls or map reading?

    a)   Yes

    b)   No

Answer: A

9. While driving, will you avoid playing loud music?

    a)   Yes

    b)   No

Answer: A

10. Will you use your turn signals every time you turn or change lanes?

    a)   Yes

    b)   No

Answer: A

11. Do you plan to cover the brake when you identify hazards that are reducing your reaction time?

a) Yes

b) No

Answer A

12. Will you try as much as possible to keep your eyes moving constantly scanning the road ahead and your mirrors for hazards?

a) Yes

b) No

Answer: A

13. Will you use your high-beam headlights whenever possible driving at night?

a) Yes

b) No

Answer: A

14. Will you make it a habit to come to a complete stop at all stop signs

a) Yes

b) No

15. Are you going to avoid returning inappropriate gestures to other drivers in all situations?

a) Yes

b) No

16. Are you willing to try to yield to faster traffic by moving to the right?

a) Yes

b) No

17. Are you going to maintain a large following distance at all times?

a) Yes

b) No

Answer: A

18. Will you use your headlights in all low visibility conditions?

    a)   Yes

    b)   No

Answer: A

19. Will you try to follow the right-of-way rules at 4 way stop signs and intersection?

    a)   Yes

    b)   No

Answer: A

20. Will you avoid talking on the phone and texting while driving?

    a)   Yes

    b)   No

Answer: A

21. Will you avoid putting yourself in a situation where you end up drinking and driving?

    a)   Yes

    b)   No

Answer: A

Chapter Three

Practice permits Test 2 (Answer Yes /No

1. It is better to change direction to the right instead of toward oncoming traffic to prevent a crash.

    a)   True

    b)   False

Answer: A

2. A cross buck or a white X shaped sign that says Railroad Crossing on it has the same meaning as a stop sign.

    a)   True

b) False

3. It is lawful to park close to a fire hydrant as long as you move your vehicle if necessary

   a) True

   b) False

4. When you are driving a motor vehicle, both hands should be on the steering wheel at all times unless you are texting.

   a) True

   b) False

5. Speaking on a cell phone while driving do increase your chances of being in a crash by as much as four times?

   a) True

b) False

6. If you want to pass a vehicle traveling in the same direction, you should pass on the left?

a) True

b) False

7. It is okay to pass another vehicle stopped for pedestrians in a crosswalk.

a) True

b) False

8. Is it lawful to give way to traffic on your right already in the roundabout?

a) True

b) False

9. After consuming alcohol, drinking coffee or a cold shower will lower your blood alcohol content.

  a) True

  b) False

Answer: B

10. Is it legal to double park in in any situations.

  a) True

  b) False

Answer: B

11. When you miss your exit on a freeway it is legal to stop and back up on the shoulder.

  a) True

  b) False

Answer: B

12. Do broken yellow lines separate lanes of traffic going in the same direction?

  a) True

b) False

13. In fog, snow and heavy rain you are obliged to use high beam lighting.

a) True

b) False

Answer: A

14. Safety belts can aid you to keep control of your car?

a) True

b) False

Answer: A

Chapter Four

Practice Permit Text 3

1. When is it lawful to drive a vehicle in a bicycle lane?

a) At most 200 feet when preparing to turn.

b) If your hazard lights are on.

c) If there are no bikes.

d) It is never lawful to drive a vehicle in a bicycle lane.

2. When is U-turn in business area legal?

a) It is legal whenever approaching vehicles are not hazardous

b) It is legal only at the intersection, unless stated otherwise

c) It is by no means legal

d) None of the above

3. How many feet before you intend to turn should you signal?

a) 25 feet.

b) 50 feet.

c) 75 feet.

d) 100 feet.

4. A driver is moving towards an intersection and observes that the traffic light is green and wants to drive straight through. Meanwhile, another vehicle is already in the intersection making a left turn. Who has the right-of-way?

a) The driver who wants to drive straight.

b) The driver who is turning left.

Answer B

5. When experiencing glare from drivers headlights at night you should?

a) Look above their headlights.

b) Look below their headlights.

c) Look in the direction of the right edge of your lane.

d) Look toward the left edge of your lane.

Answer C

6. What does a red painted curb mean?

a) Loading zone.

b) It is reserved for passenger pick up or drop off.

c) No parking or stopping.

Answer C

7. What does this hand signal mean?

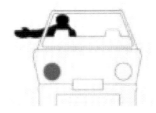

a) Left Turn.

b) Right ,Turn.

c) Stop or Slowing Down.

d) Backing.

Answer A

8. You should at no time place an infant or small child in the front seat of a vehicle with airbags

a) True

b) False

Answer A

9. **Most rear-end collisions are as a result of the vehicle in the back following too closely.**

    a)   True

    b)   False

Answer A

10. **When are you supposed to obey a construction flagger's instructions?**

    a)   When it necessary to do so.

    b)   If they do not conflict with current signs or signals.

    c)   If they are wearing a state badge.

    d)   At all times in construction zones.

Answer D

11. **When you keep your eyes locked straight ahead, is it a good defensive driving practice?**

    a)   True

    b)   False

Answer B

12. Do broken yellow lines separate lanes of traffic moving in the same direction?

    a)   True

    b)   False

Answer B

13. Pavement line colors show if you are on a one-way or two-way roadway.

    a)   True

    b)   False

Answer A

14. What does this hand signal mean?

    a)   Left turn.

    b)   Right turn.

    c)   Stop or slowing down.

d) Backing.

e) None of the above.

15 When should you use the horn?

a) To notify a vehicle to get out of your way.

b) To warning bike riders that you are passing.

c) When changing lanes quickly.

d) To prevent a possible accident.

e) To let someone know you are angry.

f) All of the above.

16. An impairment caused by a full 24 hours of being awake is nearly equal to that of the alcohol content of what?

a) .02

b) .05

c) .08

d) .10

17 When a vehicle is heading toward you in your lane, you should turn to the left.

    a) True

    b) False

18. Besides helping you with your vision at night, headlights help other people see you at any time.

    a) True

    b) False

Chapter Five

Know your Road Sign

(56 Questions and Answers)

1. What does this sign mean?

a)   Go, yield or stop

b)   Yield

c)   Stop ahead

d)   Signal ahead

Answer D

2. What does this sign means

a) General sign for a library

b) General sign for a school

c) General sign for a bus stop

d) General sign for a park

Answer A

3. Which of the sign below is not a route?

a) Sign A

b) Sign B

c) Sign C

d) None of the above

Answer C

4. What does this sign mean

a) A two way intersection ahead

b) A four way intersection ahead

c) Side road intersection ahead

d) T road intersection ahead

5. **What does this sign mean?**

a) Warning sign.

b) Regulatory sign.

c) Construction sign.

d) Guide sign.

6. **Yellow signs that have black lettering like this picture are called regulatory signs.**

a) True

b) False

Answer B

7. What does this sign mean?

a) Two way traffic advance warning

b) Winding road advance warning

c) Warning of divided high road ends ahead

d) Warning of divided highway begins ahead

Answer D

8.What does this sign mean

a) Eat if you are hungry.

b) No silverware beyond this point.

c) Food is available at the next exit.

d) This is just highway art.

9. What does this sign mean?

a) Snow removal ahead

b) Road construction flagger ahead

c) There are road workers in or near the roadway

d) Pedestrian crossing ahead

10. What does this sign means

a) Look to your right.

b) Stop if turning right.

c) Curve to the right.

d) A sharp turn to the right.

Answer C

11. What does this sign means

a) No parking allowed

b) No Passing allowed

c) No pedestrian traffic

d) No playing in the traffic

Answer A

12. Arrange these signs above in proper order from left to right.

a) Guide, warning, stop.

b) Regulatory, service, stop.

c) Regulatory, guide, stop..

d) Warning, guide, stop.

Answer D

13. What does this sign mean?

a) Divided highway

b) Left lane ends

c) Keep to the right obstruction

d) Keep to the left obstruction

Answer C

14. Is sign B a speed limit sign

a) True

b) False

15. What does this sign mean?

a) Complete stop at the sign and yield right of way to the traffic

b) Wrong way do not enter

c) Slow down your vehicle, completely stop if required, yield right of way to the traffic

d) Slow down for an approaching intersection

16. What does this sign mean?

a) Construction worker.

b) Pedestrian crossing.

c) School crossing.

d) Jogging path.

Answer C

17. What does this sign mean?

a) Winding road use caution

b) Merging traffic from the right

c) Slippery when wet use caution

d) Sharp left curve then a right curve

Answer C

18. Arrange these signs in the proper order from left to right

a)   Construction, school crossing, yield.

b)   Pedestrian crossing, construction, no passing.

c)   School crossing, construction, yield.

d)   School crossing, construction, no passing.

19. What does this sign mean

a)   Soft shoulder warning

b)   Merging traffic from the right

c)   Left lane ends ahead

d)   Narrow bridge ahead

20. What does this sign mean

a) Road splits

b) Yield

c) Merge

d) Divided highway

Answer C

21. What does this warning sign mean?

a) The road ahead curves shapely right then left

b) The road ahead turns sharply left

c) The road ahead has a sharp left curves before right curve.

d) Winding road ahead

Answer C

22. What does this bicycle sign mean?

a)   Bicycles race starts here.

b)   No bicycles.

c)   Bicycle crossing.

d)   Bicycles must park by the arrow.

Answer C

23. What does this sign means

a)   Divided traffic begins

b)   Two- way traffic ahead

c) Divided traffic ends

d) One- way traffic ahead

Answer B

24. What does this sign mean

a) Road splits

b) Merge

c) Divided highway

d) Right lane ends

Answer D

25. What does this sign means

a) Highway route sign

b) Service sign for a highway

c) Service sign for a hotel

d) Service sign for a hospital

Answer C

26. Which of these sign means two- way traffic

a) A.

b) B.

c) C.

d) None of the above.

Answer C

27. What does this sign mean?

a) Warning in advance of a low speed sharp left curve.

b) warning of a winding road

c) Road curves right then turn left

d) Advance warning of a left curve

Answer A

28. These three signs mean yield

a) True

b) False

Answer A

29. What does this sign means

a) No left turn

b) Left lane ends

c) No left lane

d) U- turn is prohibited

30. Which one of the following is found on the back of a slow moving vehicle

a) A.

b) B.

c) C.

d) None of the above.

31. What does this sign means

Slow down and yield to an oncoming vehicle

Stop only to avoid an accident

Come to a total stop; proceed only when safe to do so.

Slow down and proceed if traffic allows

Answer C

32. Which of the sign is a construction sign?

a) A.
b) B.
c) C.
d) None of the above.

Answer D

33. What does this sign means

a) There is an Intersection warning ahead, roadway ends and must turn right or left

b) Side road intersection ahead

c) Y intersection ahead

d) 4- Way intersection ahead

Answer A

34. This sign warns that you should

a) Hurry and pass someone.

b) Pass only in an emergency.

c) Never pass.

d) Pass on the left.

Answer C

35. What does this sign means

a)   End of road construction

b)   Road construction detour to the left

c)   Road construction detour to the right

d)   There is flagger ahead to control road user

Answer D

36. Which of these sign indicates do not enter?

a)   A.

b)   B.

c)   C.

d)   None of the above.

Answer B

37. What does this sign mean

Service sign for a pharmacy

Service sign for a hospital

Service sign for a doctor's office

Service sign for parking

Answer A

38. What does this sign means

a) A.

b) B.

c) C.

d) None of the above.

Answer A

39. Is it okay to go 5mph over most speed limit signs

a) True

b) False

Answer B

40. What does this sign means

a) No hunting is allowed

b) Deer crossing ahead

c) State park area

d) Wild reserve area

Answer B

41. What does this sign mean

a) If the light is red, make sure that the road is clear then you can turn.

b) No turning on green or red.

c) Make sure that the road is clear and if it happens that the light is red, and then you can turn.

d) None of the above.

Answer A

42. What does this sign mean?

a) Burning building ahead.

b) A fire truck could be entering the road ahead.

c) A truck is blocking the road.

d) There are no trucks ahead.

Answer B

43. What does this sign mean

a) V intersection ahead

b) A sharp left curve warning

c) 2 lane traffic ahead

d) A sharp right curve or turn

Answer **D**

44. What does this sign mean?

a) Runaway trucks.

b) Hill.

c) Truck parked on right triangle ahead.

d) Truck crossing.

Answer **B**

Chapter Six

Teens drivers Safety

1. More than 63 percent of teenage passenger deaths in 2008 occurred in vehicles driven by another teenager.

    a)   True

    b)   False

Answer A

2. The major cause of death for teens in the US?

    a)   Cancer

    b)   Suicide

    c)   Auto crashes

    d)   Murder

Answer C

3. Teenagers of the age 16 to 19 are how many times more likely than drivers 20 and over to be in a fatal crash.

a) 0

b) 1

c) 4

Answer A

4. The vehicle death rate for teen male drivers and passengers is practically twice that of females.

a) True

b) False

Answer A

5. Which of the age group that has a higher risk of vehicle crash over all other group are?

a) 16 to 19

b) 20 to 22

c) 23 to 25

d) Age does not matter

Answer

6. 22 percent of drivers between the age of 15 and 20 involved in fatal crashes were drinking in 2010

    a)   True

    b)   False

Answer A

7. Teens seat belt usage are very low compared to other age groups.

    a)   True

    b)   False

Answer A

Chapter Seven

Conclusion

Testing Approach

- Here are the simple tips to pass your DMV with easy
- Get yourselves Prepare in Advance by reading the entire practice test. questions
- Make sure you have an excellent night sleep.
- Do not stay more than necessary in one question
- Make sure you answer the easy questions first and go back to the unanswered or hard questions letter.
- Do not leave any question blank; always make an educated guess on each question.
- You should study the road signs test and know it by heart

About the Author

Wince. N. George is a well-known DMV text instructor with over 20 years of experience.

58123377R00044

Made in the USA
Middletown, DE
04 August 2019